Robert Teh Kok Hua

Knowledge Application In Three Steps

[Demonstrated with a Business Card (Mahjong) Game]

Gotham Books

30 N Gould St.
Ste. 20820, Sheridan, WY 82801
https://gothambooksinc.com/

Phone: 1 (307) 464-7800

© 2023 *Kok Hua Robert Teh*. All rights reserved.

No part of this book may be reproduced, stored in a retrieval system, or transmitted by any means without the written permission of the author.

Published by Gotham Books (January 3, 2024)

ISBN: 979-8-88775-518-2 (H)
ISBN: 979-8-88775-516-8 (P)
ISBN: 979-8-88775-517-5 (E)

Because of the dynamic nature of the Internet, any web addresses or links contained in this book may have changed since publication and may no longer be valid.

The views expressed in this work are solely those of the author and do not necessarily reflect the views of the publisher, and the publisher hereby disclaims any responsibility for them.

FOREWORD

By looking at the screaming international news headlines alone, it is a no brainer to see that people are fighting everywhere over limited resources be it energy (oil), food, fresh air, water, electricity and sanitation etc.

The ongoing conflicts and wars are fueling the pace for disasters including inflations of basic necessities and possibly annihilation of the human race.

Yet, the logical question that may be asked is what could international community of nations, governments, productivity agencies and news media do about it other than trading more excuses, suspicions and mutual accusations, The number of books and thesis on productivity, leadership, meritocracy, ISO standards and good corporate governance alone are simply mind-boggling for any government/productivity agencies to ever contemplate putting any of them into implementation.

For as long as the international community, governments and productivity agencies remain contented with the status quo, there is no sign of change in the horizon to say the least.

The ultimate solution clearly calls for remaking of the institutions including productivity/ISO Standards, agencies, educators in terms of (1) Leveraging of our limited resources, (2) knowledge application, (turning knowledge into products/services), (3) exercising non-technical commonsense intuition and (4) strategies for serving the masses and creating jobs as elaborated in this book. Incidentally, these four major tasks of governments may be demonstrated/practised with the help of a simple Objective-Steps Processing (OSP) Business Card (Mahjong) Game (see Appendix B).

The author is pleased to take this opportunity to commend a National Productivity Day (as prompted by his literary agent Gotham Books) in collaboration with National Productivity Associations in recognition of their contributions to productivity measures such as contained in "Knowledge Application In Three Steps". (Enquiries/ideas are welcome at roberttehkh@yahoo.com)

Teh Kok Hua

CONTENTS

CHAPTER ONE

INTRODUCTION.. 2

CHAPTER TWO

FRAMEWORK OF OSP KNOWLEDGE APPLICATION... 4

CHAPTER THREE

OVERCOMING CONCEPTUAL MINDSET... 5

CHAPTER FOUR

DEFINITION OF TASK 8

CHAPTER FIVE

AUTO-FILING TASK_CODE AND TASK-LINE 14

CHAPTER SIX

SCOPE OF KNOWLEDGE APPLICATION 16

CHAPTER SEVEN

FOUR MAJOR TASKS... 19

CHAPTER EIGHT

ROLES OF INTERNATIONAL ORGANIZATIONS 20

CHAPTER NINE

PRE-EXISTING PRODUCTIVITY METHODOLOGIES 21

CHAPTER TEN

SECRETS OF SUCCESSFUL CHIEF EXECUTIVES...22

APPENDIX A

KNOWLEDGE IN SCIENCE 23

APPENDIX B

OSP BUSINESS CARD (MAHJONG) GAME RULES 33

APPENDIX C

OSP TASK-LINE TEMPLATE 44

PART ONE

CHAPTER ONE

INTRODUCTION

Generally speaking, when people talk about success, they are likely to refer to winning in personal or business ventures with some secret recipe such as the Sun Tzu Art of War: (1) Wisdom (2) Trust (3) Courage (4) Compassion and (5) Discipline. This book will go straight into showing how to apply this common secret recipe to win in ventures, business or government.

However, as human being, we are born with an intuitive survival instinct to preserve and protect our own self-interests. Thus, in reality, useful concepts like wisdom, trust etc. are inextricably interwoven with and confounded by our own egoistic mindset. Moreover, there are other paths to success e.g., integrity, intelligence and energy (Warren Buffett) or intuitive leadership, passion, curiosities, meritocracy, talent, productivity, creativity, innovation etc.

Be it as it may, as its title suggests, this book will present a three-steps executable process to help people firstly to circumvent our egoistic mindset and secondly apply abstract concepts in three steps of administration to turn knowledge into tangible products and services.

According to the Advanced Oxford Learners' Dictionary, knowledge includes facts, information, and skills acquired through experience or education. To begin with, knowledge is not just plain facts or data. It is largely abstract and multidimensional transcending both the physical (5%) and the unknown and

PART ONE

invisible universe (95%) as elaborated in Appendix A. The prevailing belief is that the universe is ruled by energy according to Einstein Energy Equation: E=MC**2 and its the energy-gravitation- spacetime conception. There is a widely held belief as postulated by Max Planck regarded as one of the three fathers of Quantum Mechanics that all matters originated and existed by virtue of a force. Well, if there is such a force ruling the universe, it is logical to ask: What kind of force is it? What makes it so powerful to originate matter? What other powers has the force possessed? Is there such a force functioning within our being? More importantly, how can we work with this rather abstract force in particular to render concepts in Sun Tzu Art of War like wisdom, trust, courage, compassion and discipline executable. (Read Appendix A)

The three-steps knowledge application process was first published by the author in "Objective-steps Processing Management System" (OSP) in 2001. (ISBN: 981-04-6973-X) and subsequently in, "Change - Just Do It" (ISBN: 9781504339926) and "A Layman's View of The Universe" (ISBN: 9781519385499). The idea of three-steps management is nothing new. If we are to examine a notice or minutes of a corporate meeting, we will be able to verify that businesses are commonly transacted with logic and common sense in agenda (proposal) enquiry (study, quotation, tender) and contract (results) steps.

At this point, it is pertinent to reiterate that the raison d'état in any business or government is to win. Clearly, the most practical way to win is through getting things done in executable processes without being bogged down in circuitous concepts and technological technicalities.

CHAPTER TWO

FRAMEWORK OF OSP KNOWLEDGE APPLICATION

Objective-steps Processing (OSP) by which the three-steps knowledge application is referred to in this book essentially translates Objects to discrete Steps to render fuzzy tasks executable. The stepwise method has come a long way from its atomism approach having been fine-tuned, and successfully tested in diverse work environments over twenty plus years with the extraordinary efficacies as shown in the following OSP Framework:

Simplicity - By correlating abstract concepts to steps/departmental core tasks, we are rendering fuzzy tasks executable in three steps of administration and ten departments of operation with result-targeting closure via the unique OSP one-liner task-lines.

Consistency and focus - By monitoring performance and correction of variances of four major tasks in knowledge application via the one-liner result-targeting task-lines.

Non-theoretical and non-technical.

Teamwork. (Balance)

Thus, as can be seen from the above-stated OSP Framework, fuzzy tasks are rendered executable in steps-core task processes with a closure by the unique one-liner result-targeting task-lines. More importantly it is in accord with the law of nature or the Tao intrinsically functioning within our being - balancing or exchange of benefits.

CHAPTER THREE

OVERCOMING CONCEPTUAL MINDSET

Before going further, let us briefly recapitulate why businesses and governments have been calling for a change of mindset or thinking out of the box without much success for decades. The main reason is the lack of productivity, and abuses and malpractices associated with conventional conceptual, ad hoc and fire-fight management practices. To be sure, concepts like leadership and creativity, meritocracy etc. can be useful for presentation and understanding of problems and issues. They include any form or collection of ideas and principles. According to Lao Tzu, the ancient political philosopher of China whom even the venerable Confucius had consulted, all things are governed by the law of nature known as the Tao, functioning with balancing between Yin (negative) and Yang (positive) elements called "chi", meaning that people ought to live with moderation - avoiding excesses, luxury and bigness. But make no mistake: the Tao is not just a concept. It is a law of nature functioning within our being responsible for our living in good health, peace and harmony.

Given the overwhelming evidence of an abstract force ruling the universe and our being as elaborated in Appendix A, it makes sense to rethink knowledge in science. More importantly, it is an opportunity for us to harness the force or Tao within us to reap the biggest benefits through knowledge application.

PART ONE

There is no doubt that while technical or technological knowledge such as properties of materials or software and hardware engineerings are critical, they are not enough to help us get things done productively. It is through teamwork fostered by abstract concepts like Wisdom, Trust, Courage, Compassion and Discipline derived from the Tao within us - balancing Yin and Yang "chi" for exchange of benefits - that we are best able to succeed in our ventures. See the Tao-like OSP Logo on the front cover signified by the outer loop (the Force) and inner double loops, (the Yin and Yang balance).

For evidence of such a Tao law of nature functioning within our being, readers may also refer to the biological science where it is well established that our brain is balanced by the left and right hemispheres. Our heart is functioning too with a positive-negative Cardiac Conduction System. Our neuron network too are functioning on such an overall balance.

It goes without saying that a choice has to be made by any one whether or not to work with the intrinsic Tao within our being. One thing is certain though. Being ignorant or working against the Tao, there are consequences. By working with the Tao, we are obviously better able to avoid causing unnecessary stress to our health with all the bad habits like procrastination, compromises, complacencies, justifications, hypocrisies, excuses, abuses and malpractices.

Moreover, as stated in an old Chinese adage: "adversities spell opportunities". Thus, through working with the Tao, we are opening many windows of opportunities out there to turn knowledge into winning products and services.

PART TWO

CHAPTER FOUR

DEFINITION OF TASK

As anyone familiar with computer science may be able to testify, a task is invariably defined as a class object set by its own in-built constructor, methods and attributes. It will be noticed that in computerisation, highly fuzzy and technical tasks are nevertheless rendered executable by its in-built constructor and processed with a closing to its zero state - in line with the Tao too.

To cut the long story short, OSP knowledge application is simply a matter of subtly swapping our egoistic conceptual mindset for user-friendly result-targeting executable knowledge application processes and correction of variances via the compendious one-liner task lines as shown by the following quick-example task-lines:

QUICK EXAMPLE TASK-LINES:

1_4_1_0.agenda_invest_stock_X.A_PE_NTA_ trend_$n.

1_4_2_0.agenda_DB_X.A_ stock_n_yield%

1_4_3_0.agenda_matter_arising_X.A_n

1_4_4_0.agenda_proj_X.A_cost_$n

PART TWO

2_4_1_0.enq_X.A_ quotation_$n

2_4_2_0.enq_DB_X.A_$n

2_4_3_0.enq_X.A_$

2_4_4_0.enq_proj_X.A_ bridge_cost_$n.

3_4_1_0.cont_X.A_$

3_4_2_0.cont_DB_X.A_$

3_4_3_0.cont_V.A_ decision

3_4_4_0.cont_proj_X.A_ item

From these quick example task-lines, we can see the Tao as a "constructor" of sorts or alter ego bridging the three steps of administration (i.e., agenda, enquiry and contracts) and the results-targeting task-lines. In other words, the Tao is always with us. It is up to us to exercise its intrinsic wisdom, trust, courage, compassion and discipline in getting things done productively

All it takes in knowledge application is simply to structure tasks in steps-core task executable processes and to close the task-lines with teamwork and results. The possibilities are endless. Read the knowledge application processes in science to better understand why tasks need to be closed based on logics and common sense as elaborated in Appendix A. The three steps of administration are supported by facts and data from the Ten Departments of Operation namely: (1) Accounts (2) Enforcement (3) Facility (4) General (5) Human Resource (6) Marketing (7) Production (8) Regulation (9) Revenue and (10) Services.

Each step and department are designated with four core tasks (See Core Task Table in Appendix C) to render fuzzy tasks executable via the core tasks we are familiar with. There may be differences of perception on what our core tasks should be. Nevertheless, with training, and practice of the Business Card Game, staff will get to know instinctively that these step-correlated core tasks (see Appendix C) enable them to follow through productive execution of any tasks naturally upon any decision/policy made.

The four-digit task code preceding the task-lines serves as an auto-filing and quick retrieval aid which is already a big step towards productivity.

The first digit (1, 2, 3, or 4) of the task code points to the relevant object namely 1: Agenda, 2: Enquiry, 3: Contract, and 4: Operations. The second digit stands for the "Attribute A" linking to the actual task via the core task (first, second, third or fourth).

The last digit '0' or '1' is for closing of the status: variance or closed tasks respectively. Thus, at a glance, of the task-line, staff will know their core tasks instinctively and what to do to execute the actual task to close it (e.g., 2_4_1_1.enq_quotation. item_$n.) guided by the task code with updating of its status from '0' to digit '1'.

PART TWO

It is important to note that the steps and core tasks are our pre-existing duties and not extra burden imposed on staff like the numerous standard operating procedures, ISO standards, the Six Sigma, Competency/Mind Mapping routines or a whole lot of professional codes of practices etc.

The ultimate of productivity in OSP therefore lies in self-evident result-targeted closing.

With the help of the self-explanatory result-targeting task-lines, anyone could be easily trained to get started on knowledge application.

To recapitulate, as long as the task-lines are being closed with self-evident results, the enterprise is in effect exercising concepts of wisdom, trust, courage, compassion and discipline of Sun Tzu Art of War recipe of success. For example, in OSP, compassion is engendered by training, motivation and career development while discipline by targeted results. Wisdom, Trust and Courage are exercised through overall guidance, direction and responsibility. Instead of talking about conceptual leadership, creativity, meritocracy, talent etc., OSP establishes a connectivity to the Tao functioning within us to the three steps of administration as a "constructor" of sorts via teamwork, executable processes and self-evident results.

For students, coping to learn the mountains of knowledge, it is easy to get distracted from their final goal - knowledge application. The self-explanatory task-lines should be simple enough to guide them on how to apply concepts and theories learned in studies proactively and get started on knowledge application. Hopefully, educators and students can see for themselves the blind spots that have prevented them from reaching their full potential in the past the alternative would be getting stuck in the status quo, slogging for jobs, examinations or grades meaninglessly for more decades to come.

A good start in knowledge application is to train a junior staff as "enforcer" to maintain integrity of syntax and execution processes. For example, the enforcer could set up a core task table to help staff in the Facility Department: to follow through its first core task: Inspection, to detect and rectify faults with corrective actions to ensure smooth operation of facilities without further instruction.

In the same way, staff within the Production Department will know their First Core task with which to work as a team to achieve winning products within competitive costs. Scientists, researchers and even sports men and women should be able to see that their talent per se is not enough. It needs to be made executable via the steps and core tasks fostered by the Tao within us by the whole team for talent to bloom. The task-lines may be displayed in an inner office, to assist the chief executive in coordinating the team in calling quotations or seeking resource or technical solutions. The chief executive does not really need to be overly concerned with the details of execution. All he needs to do is to be an enlightened servant leader to let the team deliver their best results through knowledge application via teamwork. Detailed explanations of how the task-lines work in practice are provided in the Task-line Template in Appendix C. Of course, confidential stuff, such as costs or marketing strategies could be presented separately.

PART TWO

Minor or mundane tasks like discussions, or appointments, travel etc. are non-issues as they will be taken care of by the core tasks. Unfortunately, all too often, managers or chief executives are routinely engaged in micro-managing minor issues missing the wood for the tree so to speak causing adverse office politics, compromises and malpractices.

CHAPTER FIVE

AUTO-FILING TASK_CODE AND TASK-LINE

To illustrate how the knowledge application works in practice, let us examine it with reference to the universal filing system adopted by the libraries. A visit to the libraries will without doubt reveal that books (knowledge, facts, records, files) are generally arranged based on scanty general subject headers like Health & Fitness Business & Finance, Computer & IT, Fiction and General (Non-Fiction), Recreation etc. Any casual visitors may need to go through all the shelves or seek help in order to locate the desired books outside the general headers. By upgrading the general headers to an Object- Attribute format, not only are readers better able to locate a wider scope of books, most importantly, they are ushered onto the path of knowledge application by related hardwares and softwares e.g., Education.Science_ material_specs, Education. Art_design_ genre, Education. Geography_ topography, Education. Computer_IT_python, Education. History_ Modern_China etc. In this way, library visitors, scientists, researchers, educators and students are best able to relate their academic studies to knowledge application. Moreover, the task code (e.g., 1_4_1_0) will integrate with the existing general headers by simply assigning the first digit as "0" to denote general, and third digit "n" as existing headers thus: 0_4_n_0, (say n='1' for fiction, n='2' for non-fiction or n='3' for healthcare etc.). Another problem with the general header is that a book under one general header e.g., computer IT may often be found under other general headers e.g., General (Non-Fiction) etc. Hence with this filing upgrade, the general library users, educators and students alike will be able to maximize usage of libraries for knowledge application without extra costs.

Notice that various productivity associations, and ISO code-of-practice agencies etc. have been talking about conceptual policies of all kinds like leadership, productivity, creativity, standardization and standard operating procedures for ages supposedly to improve productivity and standards of living for the masses. Despite the great volumes of Standard Operating Procedures, the ISO registrations, it remains to be seen whether any of them have become truly and universally implementable or achieved the intended productivity. There are without doubts utilitarian values with setting of standards. But whether the standards have rendered tasks recognisable or executable is a different matter. Or are they being simply complacent to rely on standards for self-promotion and advertising purposes.

CHAPTER SIX

SCOPE OF KNOWLEDGE APPLICATION

As can be seen from Appendix A, the scope of knowledge in the context of science is abstract and wide. Thus, in knowledge application, the key issue would be how to turn abstract knowledge in science into products and services to stay competitive. So, the biggest benefits of OSP would include: (1) the long-awaited universal executable productivity processes, (2) prevention of incessant facility breakdowns in public Road, Rail, Marine or Air Transportations, or major Power Supply/ Transmission Installations and (3) Avoidance of abuses and malpractices.

Practically, OSP offers an authentic and proven help to avoid the frequent cashflow problems leading to insolvency or bankruptcy. The widespread Silicon Banking crises of 2023 found to be attributable to mismanagement could have been avoided easily via the simple OSP one-liner monitoring task-lines. Perhaps the biggest lesson from the SV Banking crisis is that money cannot make money by itself or under the guise of financial engineering. Money can grow only from economic knowledge application activities. The ten checklists of OSP (part of core tasks) furthermore will help to ensure that public services like stock-market and banking regulators are themselves setting good examples of corporate governance often talked about with transparency and accountability. In administration of law and justice it is important to exercise flexibility in punishment based on facts and circumstances preempted by the checklists. The Accounts Department could simply monitor proactively via its first core task: "Posting" for proper financial control to

PART TWO

avoid the frequent malpractices and irregularities. The whole auditing process needs to be revamped to detect variances with warnings and exceptions instead of waiting till it is too late. There is no doubt that businesses and governments can and must free themselves from the hostage of the diverse unworkable conceptual approaches without any more lame excuses. Let the concepts from various researches stay as useful aid for presentation and understanding of problems but not to be mistaken as the be-all-end-all solutions to our immense human problems. With such a mindset change, the various Standard and Productivity agencies can then be upgraded to make their conceptual policies executable to target at results by the simple monitoring task-lines. Only then they can truly play a more effective role in knowledge application. For the skeptics, let there be no doubt that OSP is no easy journey. I have had to overcome my fair share of obstacles myself in my own knowledge application journey. For one thing, I did not have the benefit of pro-knowledge English education to begin with. The Chinese educated will know that apart from the deeply ingrained beneficial cultural values, the Chinese language semantics being structured in about two thousand basic image-like characters slow down learning of science. It was not easy to learn English for a non-elite Chinese educated. It was during the final years of my secondary education that I realized that in order to seek employment in an English dominated environment, I needed to switch over to English education. For another thing, being non-university trained, I have had a whale of time to catch up with my knowledge of science and engineering through my own self-study. So, for those seriously considering keeping up with the technology race, like quantum computing, they may well encounter diverse obstacles before reaching the final solution of "Change - Just Do It". Do not give up though. Start knowledge

PART TWO

application today. It will be one of the best decisions ever made for yourself, your children and the masses. The "no-nothing" alternative will mean keeping to the status quo, slogging at jobs, examinations or grades to no avail just to look good. As an added bonus, the task-lines will help all to work together as a team. The one-liner task-lines will be an effective means for remote or space-age communication.

Finally, it is important to be positive-minded, and consistent in knowledge application. One way to do so is by focusing on closing of four major tasks via the task-lines thus: e.g., 1_4_1_0 > 1_4_1_1, 1_4_2_0 > 1_4_2_1, or 4_7_3_0 > 4_7_3_1 etc. The criterion for closing of task-lines is self-evident results. Outstanding task-lines should serve as a coordinator as well as reminder to the staff concerned on what to do.

CHAPTER SEVEN

FOUR MAJOR TASKS

As mentioned in the foregoing, it is important to be consistent and focused in knowledge application by monitoring four major tasks as follows:

1) Leveraging resources.

2) Knowledge application.

3) Intuition.

4) Strategies.

(Note: Interestingly, these four major tasks can be demonstrated with the fun Business Card [Mahjong] Game - See Appendix B)

Thus, this book is set up in two parts. Part One is concerned with getting results on four major tasks. Part Two is devoted to the how-to of rendering abstract concepts executable through knowledge application processes. The professionals, scientists, engineers, researchers, accountants, lawyers, and even sports men and women should realize that no matter how talented they may be, they could only maximize their potential through teamwork by working with the Tao within them. (See examples in Appendix C).

CHAPTER EIGHT

ROLES OF INTERNATIONAL ORGANIZATIONS

In the larger perspective, national governments, businesses, United Nations, and its ISO Standards and productivity agencies, could truly see for themselves why they must change mindset once and for all without hypocrisies or lame excuses. Only then can they truly serve their stakeholders and masses. The OSP offers a ready and proven hands-on management process to help them serve the masses for progress, productivity, harmony and peace. There is no valid reason to rehash the generic leadership, rule of law, or creativity as all these concepts are interpreted differently depending on perceptions. The worse is to persist in conceptual practices for self-interests only to the seeds for human conflicts, and even wars in a zero-sum game edging mankind toward self-destruction.

CHAPTER NINE

PRE-EXISTING PRODUCTIVITY METHODOLOGIES

Despite the introduction of endless productivity methodologies like Standard Operating Procedures, ISO standards and various codes of practices, skill upgrading courses, competency schemes, mind mapping, Six Sigma, Toyota Production System (people-process connectivity) etc., it remains to be seen whether any of them have proven to be universally implementable. Despite the great number of ISO-registered enterprises, for example, it may be asked how many of them are truly productive.

As Robert K. Greenleaf had put it, proper leadership should be what he called "servant leadership" in order to get the whole team to work together to develop its best. Well, even servant leadership is just a theoretical concept. By way of another example, creativity is often held to be another common recipe of success. If we are to examine the recommended four pillars of creativity said to be rapport, acute sensory awareness, outcome thinking and behavioral flexibility defined under Neuro Linguistic programming, we will find concepts like rapport awareness hardly implementable too.

CHAPTER TEN

SECRETS OF SUCCESSFUL CHIEF EXECUTIVES

Finally, it may well be asked: What are the secrets of success of highly successful chief executives? As Jack Welch the ex-chief executive credited for bringing up General Electric from a small enterprise to the world's largest multinational corporation in the 1970s had pointed out in his book "Winning", success is always about winning; execution holds the key to success. In the same vein, Steve Jobs who was notably responsible for turning a floundering Apple Corporation around to become the world's biggest computer maker had revealed a "Product-driven" method (knowledge application) as secret of Apple's success. So here we are, the key to success as exemplified by these successful chiefs simply lies in execution and knowledge application. The OSP Knowledge Application Process as described in this book is in line with the execution and knowledge application approach of highly successful chief executives. It is moreover non-technical and non-conceptual. It offers a simple practical tool to help all concerned to reap the biggest benefits from knowledge application.

APPENDIX A

As explained in earlier chapters, it is essential in knowledge application to know what constitute knowledge. Hence this appendix is provided for this purpose in the context of science albeit from a layman's perspective. The prevailing view is that the universe is ruled by energy according to Einstein Energy Equation: E=MC**2 and his energy-gravitation- spacetime conception. Incidentally, an alternative view had been postulated by Max Planck widely regarded as one of the three fathers of quantum mechanics that all matters originated and existed by virtue of a force. The force-based view was concurred by eminent scientists like Lawrence Krauss, Stephen Hawking and Alexander Vilenkin who likened the universe as originated from nothingness. In this regard, it may be recalled that Einstein himself too had assumed a force existed in space in the form of cosmological constant. Moreover, this force-based view of the universe is highly consistent with findings under quantum mechanics of a Zero-Point Field in the vacuum of space which is highly unstable due to the Heisenberg Uncertainty Principle. Although Einstein Energy Equation, and relativity theory is holding sway in explaining the physical universe, the reality is that much of the universe such as dark energy, dark matter remain largely unknown. Various phenomena are yet to be explained by the energy or gravitational conception such as the following:

1) Although the universe is generally believed to be ruled by energy as stated in the Einstein Energy Equation: E=MC**2 and General Relativity Theory, the energy-gravitation-spacetime conception is yet to explain the 95% invisible universe - dark energy, dark matter, black holes. The assumption

that the physical part (5%) was counterbalanced by a Cosmopolitan Constant was proven wrong with the discovery of an expanding physical universe.

2) The massless Higgs Field present in every region of the universe is found capable of transforming (via bosons, gluons, quarks, strong force and weak force) to matter.

3) There existed various intent-driven phenomena e.g. creation of living things, functioning of our mind, body, heart, nervous system (connected in a neural network of neurons connected to dendritic cells transmitting signal via axion to our various organs), sexual reproduction, immunity system, migratory birds' and bees' abilities to see magnetic fields and even behaviors of plants (like the Shein creeper) to twirl its tendrils around wire ropes on its own to withstand the force of wind to name just a few.

4) The wave-like nature of particles and phenomenon of quantum entanglement experimentally proven by a team of researchers led by professor Dr. Christian Schonenbrrger and Dr. Andreas Blaumgartner in collaboration with professor Dr. Lucia Sorba from Istituto Nanoscience-CNR (Nov 23, 2023, reported in SciTechDaily) where electron of up-spin was found to be paired by one of the down-spin irrespective of distance (timeless) of separation.

5) Other unaccountable phenomena include e.g., gas molecules' behavior to separate themselves into hot and cold compartments through a hole in the central partition known as Maxwell Daemon.

6) The existence of powerful forces holding the repellent positively charged protons within the nucleus. What is the nature of the strong force holding up-quarks and down-quarks to form neutrons? Why is the gravity of neutron stars so exceptionally dense?

7) In Machine Learning, it is well established that living beings are able to adapt to change by experience.

Given the above-listed phenomena, it would seem illogical for the universe to be ruled by energy or confined to its visible physical energy-gravitation- spacetime boundary! On the other hand, as well established in Quantum Mechanics, there existed a zero-point field in the vacuum of space which is highly unstable fluctuating about its zero state with a power to revert to its nascent zero state as may be represented mathematically by the algorithm: $0= (+1) +(-1)$. Clearly, such a force of space is timeless in that it existed regardless of distance, speed of light, creation, or entropy of matter or living things. It is also quantum in nature in that its uncertainty state would logically be capable of generating a two-dimensional force and energy causing warping to the three-dimensional space collaborated by the accompanying Law of Energy Conservation throughout. The discovery of electrons of up-spin being paired by one of down-spin despite distance of separation is yet another piece of evidence pointing to the existence of the quantum force in space. Perhaps the best evidence that the universe is ruled by a quantum force is as reported by ETH ZURICH in an article by SciTechDaily dated 11/05/2023 which stated that "A team of researchers led by professor Andreas Wallraff at ETH Zurich have found that quantum objects separated by great distances are more strongly correlated than possible by Einstein's local causality". However, scientists seemed to be preoccupied with experimentally provable facts and data relating to the physical aspects like energy, gravitation, planets and galaxies, the Big Bang theory and diffusion of plasma: Cosmic Microwave Background. By so doing, they might be addressing the symptoms rather than the root causes. Additionally, time or speed of light referred to in Einstein's general relativity comes into relevance only in relation to entropy of things or our human existence or experience after the birth of the universe.

It is therefore logical to study the nature of the primordial quantum force of space evidenced by the Zero-point Field to see whether it is part of the intrinsic properties or attributes of the infinite expanse of space. If so, then how do we go about proving it? Perhaps, even gravity itself may not be directly derived from matter but rather from the densely packed quarks forming protons and neutrons. The resultant gravity-induced space boundary perhaps could be better attributable to the two-dimensional force that warps the three-dimensional space.

Moreover, the massless Higgs Field is found to be capable of transformation by what is known as the Higgs Mechanism to quarks and matter. Scientists believed that since the Higgs Field is massless, it is not a force which is associated with mass. If that is the case, it may be asked: where are the Higgs Mechanism or Heisenberg uncertainty from; what is the cause or causes of the wave-like nature of light/particles or Quantum Entanglement in the first place! Certainly, the Higgs Field could not just come from thin air.

Also, it is highly unlikely the mass-associated gravity is responsible for Higgs Field transformation to matter! Additionally, scientists have found that every one of the six flavors of quark (matter) created, is paired by a corresponding mirror-image antiparticle or anti-quark. Obviously, neither energy nor gravity is the cause of Higgs Field's capability to transform to matter nor matter-antimatter parity

Therefore, knowledge in science is abstract and multidimensional beyond experimentally provable facts and data.

From all this indirect evidence, there is a case for relooking at knowledge in science. For example, should we study whether the zero-point field is the generator of a two-dimensional force, causing warping to three-dimensional space, transformation of Higgs Field to matter and the matter-antimatter parity as established in the Standard Model of Physical Particles. The subsequent discoveries of anti-matters like, anti-hydrogen etc. lends further credence to the existence of a primordial force with a quantum power to revert to its nascent zero-point state. From the fact that matter created by the Higgs Field is balanced by antimatter, we can deduce a more fundamental cause at work for transformation of Higgs Field to matter, the matter-antimatter parity and electron of up-spin to be balanced by one of down-spin.

It may also be asked: what is the origin of gravity? The existing belief is that gravity is associated with matter. Considering that matter is formed by closely packed quarks as protons and neutrons, why shouldn't gravity be derived from the quarks?

It may be worthwhile to study what kind of force is binding the up and down quarks strongly together to form matter? Why is the gravity of Neutron star so dense? Is such dense gravity attributable to the closely packed quarks forming matter? In such a scenario, shouldn't the boundary of the physical universe be logically determined by the interactions between the two-dimensional force, derived from the primordial void of space, quarks and matter. The physical planets clearly could be better explained by the intersection between the two-dimensional force, and quarks rather than by energy or some mysterious spacetime or relativity. Scientists have also predicted that the gravitational forces will results in planets and galaxies collapsing into black hole in which event all information would be destroyed by the hottest of temperature. As observed by powerful telescope, black holes were found being capable of spitting out planets and galaxies. Therefore, these discoveries serve as further evidence that energy-gravitation-spacetime conception is insufficient to explain the universe. It is logical that there existed a quantum force in space with a power to create matter and antimatter as well as balancing between two-dimensional force and quarks! The physical planets, galaxies are logically likely to be in a state of balance between force, and quarks in the same way that matter is balanced by mirror-image antimatter due to the quantum power of zero-point field. Without such a zero-point quantum force, there may not be parity between matter with antimatter. There may not be energy to begin with accompanied by the pervasive law of conservation of energy. The physical universe would have collapsed a long time ago.

So instead of focusing the physical aspects of planets, galaxies black holes, Big Bang theory, singularity, spacetime or plasma cosmic microwaves, there is a case for studying what is the nature of the primordial quantum zero-point field. How does it keep balancing between positives and negatives, matter and antimatter? The main issue facing science today is that energy and gravitational conception alone is insufficient to explain phenomena like the Quantum Entanglement, or transformation of the massless Higgs Field to matter, matter-antimatter parity or existence of dark energy and dark matter, and also the intent-driven behaviors among living being.

By studying the formation of elements as shown in the Periodic Table, we can see more evidence of intent-driven behaviours. The contiguous arrangement of protons within the nucleus leaving no gap in such proton configuration between two adjacent atoms is clearly such an intent-driven behavior. What could be the cause of such intent-driven behaviours? It is not unreasonable to surmise that the negative-positive polarities are the cause for lightning (powerful forces from the Zero-point field) and magnetism that keep the planets in rotations. It is also likely to be the cause of such intent-driven proton configuration and formation of chemicals and compounds to create and sustain lives.

Some scientists have argued that the Zero-Point Field was not significant enough to account for the total energy content of the universe. But these scientists obviously failed to see that the primordial space is infinite and could not possibly be the same as the near-zero field state after the birth of the universe. Any quantification of space energy after the birth of the physical universe could not possibly be equated to that of before as a substantial part of the primordial force of space would have already been converted to matter.

Scientists have reasoned that during the hottest part of the Big Bang, all laws have broken down. If so, what could have happened during or after the hottest temperature of the Big Bang? Surely the law of conservation of energy has existed throughout as it could not just disappeared and reappeared on its own. An additional issue is: What is a singularity?

Therefore, from our above-elaborated brief review of knowledge in science, we can see that knowledge is abstract and multidimensional.

Hence, given the overwhelming scientific evidence of existence of a largely unknown uncertain zero-point field, it is logical to rethink the existing experimentally based energy-gravitation-spacetime theory.

Perhaps, the best advice is from Einstein himself when he regarded gravity as being balanced by a force from space. Clearly his view of a cosmological constant is largely logical or common sense. It can be seen that while scientific experimentation is critical, it is not the be-all-end-all of knowledge. Logic and common sense (Intuition) do play just an equally important part in knowledge acquisition and application.

The only issue to be resolved would be what is the nature and power of the that largely unknown primordial zero-point field. Is it a property or attribute of the infinite expanse of space?

In summing up, there is overwhelming indirect evidence that knowledge in science is abstract and multidimensional. There existed overwhelming evidence that the universe is ruled by:

a) A force as evidenced by the uncertain zero-point field that logically existed in the primordial void as part of the intrinsic properties of infinite expanse of space

b) The existence of the Zero-point field is consistent with findings under the quantum mechanics of a zero-point energy in space which is highly unstable fluctuating according to the Heisenberg Uncertainty Principle with an intrinsic power to revert to its nascent zero-point state.

c) Such a quantum force is logically capable of imparting a two-dimensional force and energy causing warping to the three-dimensional space regarded by Einstein as spacetime boundary.

d) The existence of the quantum space force is collaborated by the Higgs Field's transformation to matter.

e) The quantum force of space is present everywhere including the interior of atoms and nucleus as evidenced by the strong binding power of closely packed (glued) quarks within neutrons and protons. The extraordinary binding power of quarks may possibly be evidenced by the exceptionally powerful gravity of neutron stars.

f) Gravity itself may possibly be attributable to the strong binding power of quarks.

g) The quantum power of the space force is logically responsible for creation of mirror-image antimatter to balance matter.

h) The galaxies, planets, dark energy, dark matter and black holes are possibly in a state of balance between force, quarks and matter for the same reason matter is balanced by antimatter due to the quantum power of the same zero-point field to revert to its nascent zero-point state.

i) The quantum power of the primordial force logically are the cause of wavelike nature and quantum entanglement of particle/light.

Therefore, given the above-elaborated abstract and multidimensional nature of knowledge, as elaborated in Appendix A, the least we can do is to work with the force within our being. We can do well by working with the Tao thereby rendering concepts and fuzzy tasks executable through knowledge application.

This being a book on knowledge application, we will not delve too deeply into science. Suffice to say that as established in biological science, our mind and body operate like a supercomputer as explained earlier. Moreover, the intent-driven phenomena could not possibly happen on their own. They are more likely attributable to the same quantum power of space force to revert to its nascent zero state as explained in the foregoing.

APPENDIX B

BUSINESS CARD (MAHJONG) GAME

As explained in earlier chapters, in order to stay competitive in whatever is our business or venture, it is essential to turn passive knowledge into tangible products or services. By executing our core tasks in three steps of administration - agenda (proposal), enquiry (study, quotation, tender) and contract (result), - and monitoring and correcting variances via the unique one-liner result-targeting task-lines, we are in effect applying knowledge to turn it into products or services. For consistency, in knowledge application, it is essential to focus on processing of four major tasks namely (1) Leveraging on resource (2) Knowledge Application (3) Intuition and (4) Strategies.

Coincidentally, such four major tasks in OSP may be demonstrated with a fun Business Card (Mahjong) Game. Without further ado, let us play this fun game as described in below:

GAME RULES:

NUMBER OF PLAYERS:

    Two to Four

DEAL OF CARDS:

Before starting the game, players will draw a card each from the shuffled pack of 52 common playing cards; the one picking the highest-ranking card as defined in Card Table below will be the dealer. The dealer will then deal to each player and himself from the one on his left one card at a time face-down in a clockwise direction up to a total of ten cards each.

1_4_1_0.
AGENDA_X.A_

1_4_2_0.
AGENDA_DB.
MINUTES

1_4_3_0.
AGENDA_MATTER_
ARISING.A_

1_4_4_0.
AGENDA_MATTER_
PROJ.A_

2_4_1_0. ENQ_X.A_

2_4_2_0.ENQ_DB.A_

2_4_3_0.ENQ_X.A_

2_4_4_0. CHECKLIST_1. PAYMENT

3_4_1_0. CONT_X.A_

3_4_2_0. CONT_DB.A_

3_4_3_0.CONT_X.A_

3_4_4_0. CHECKLIST_2. TERMS

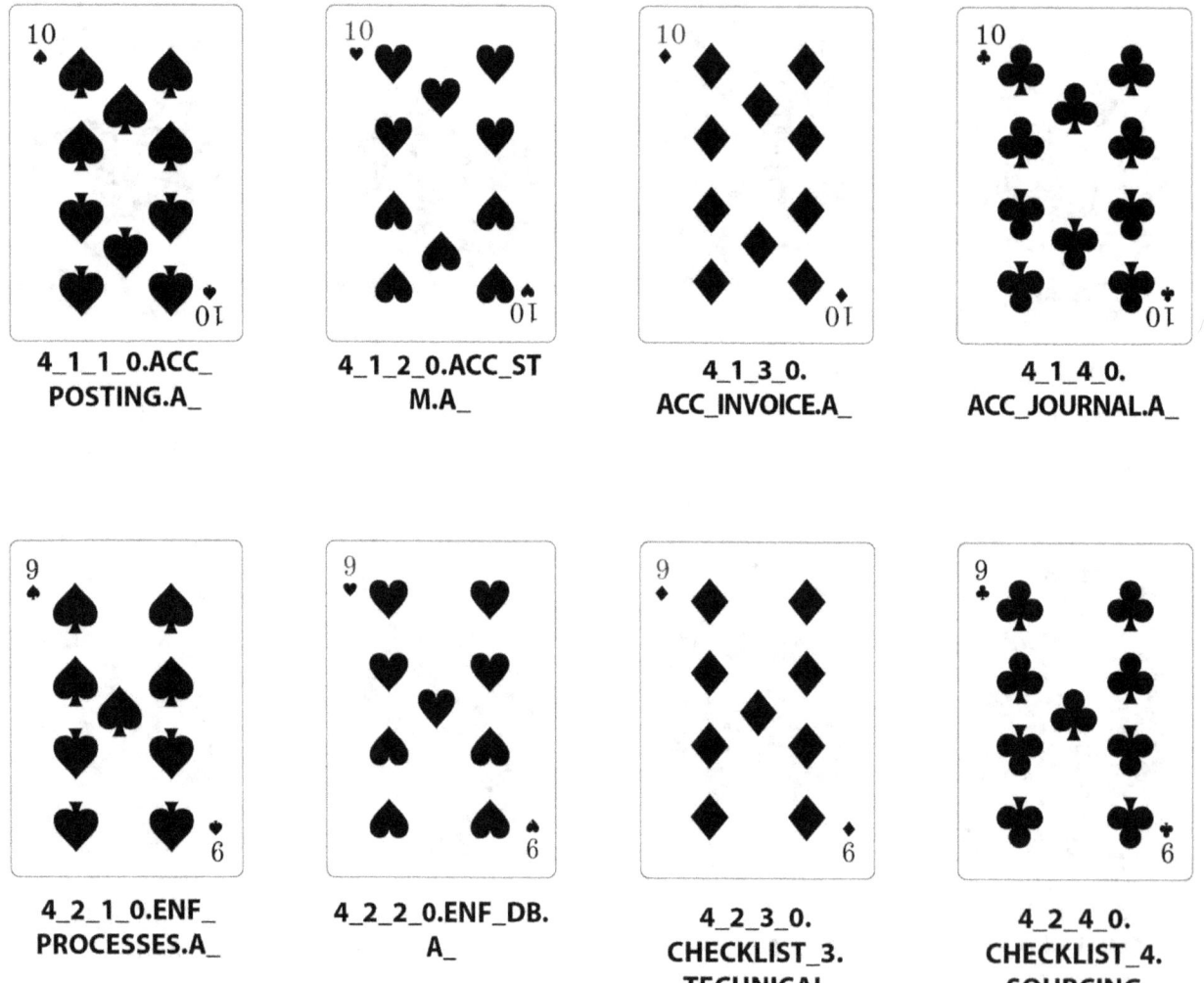

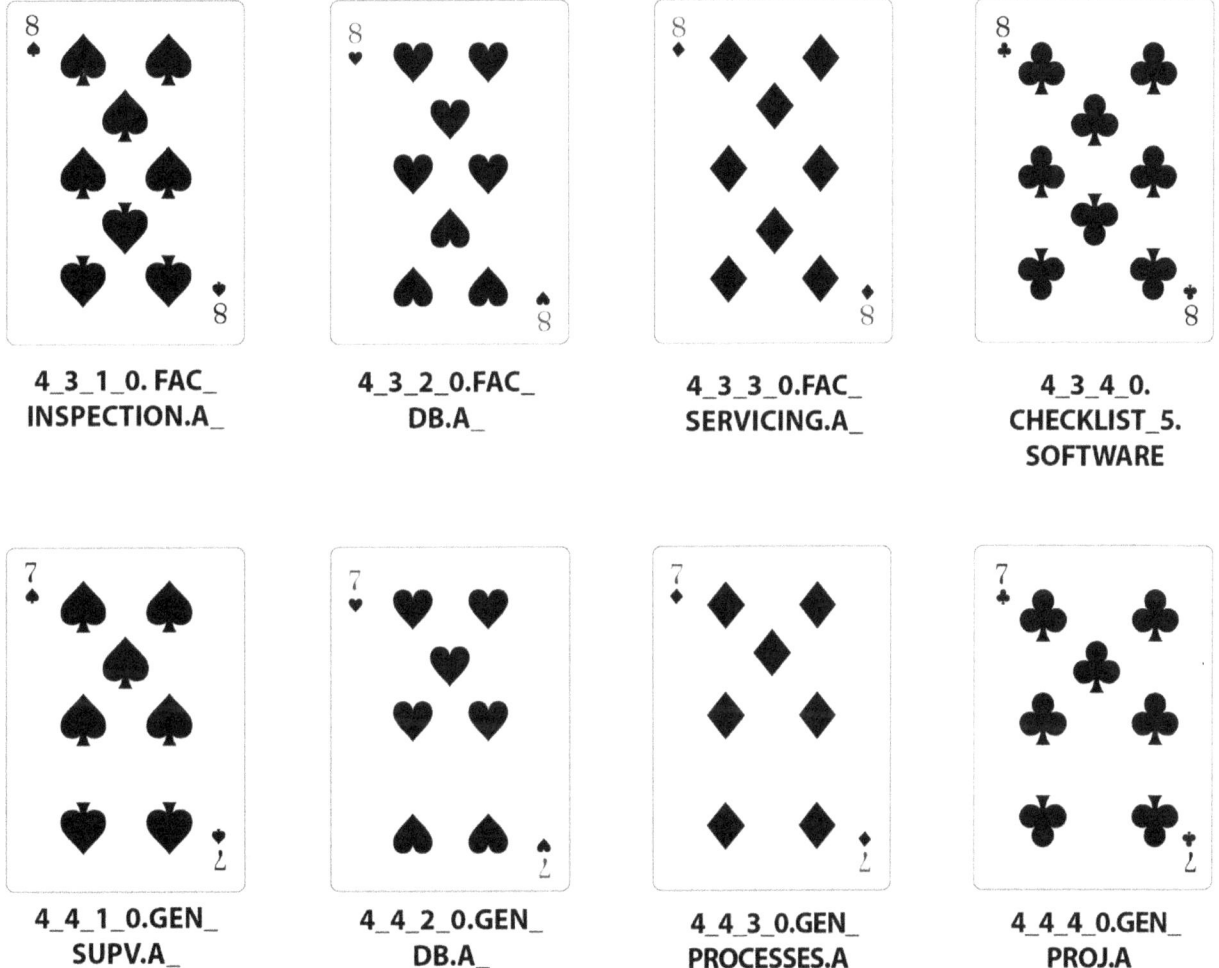

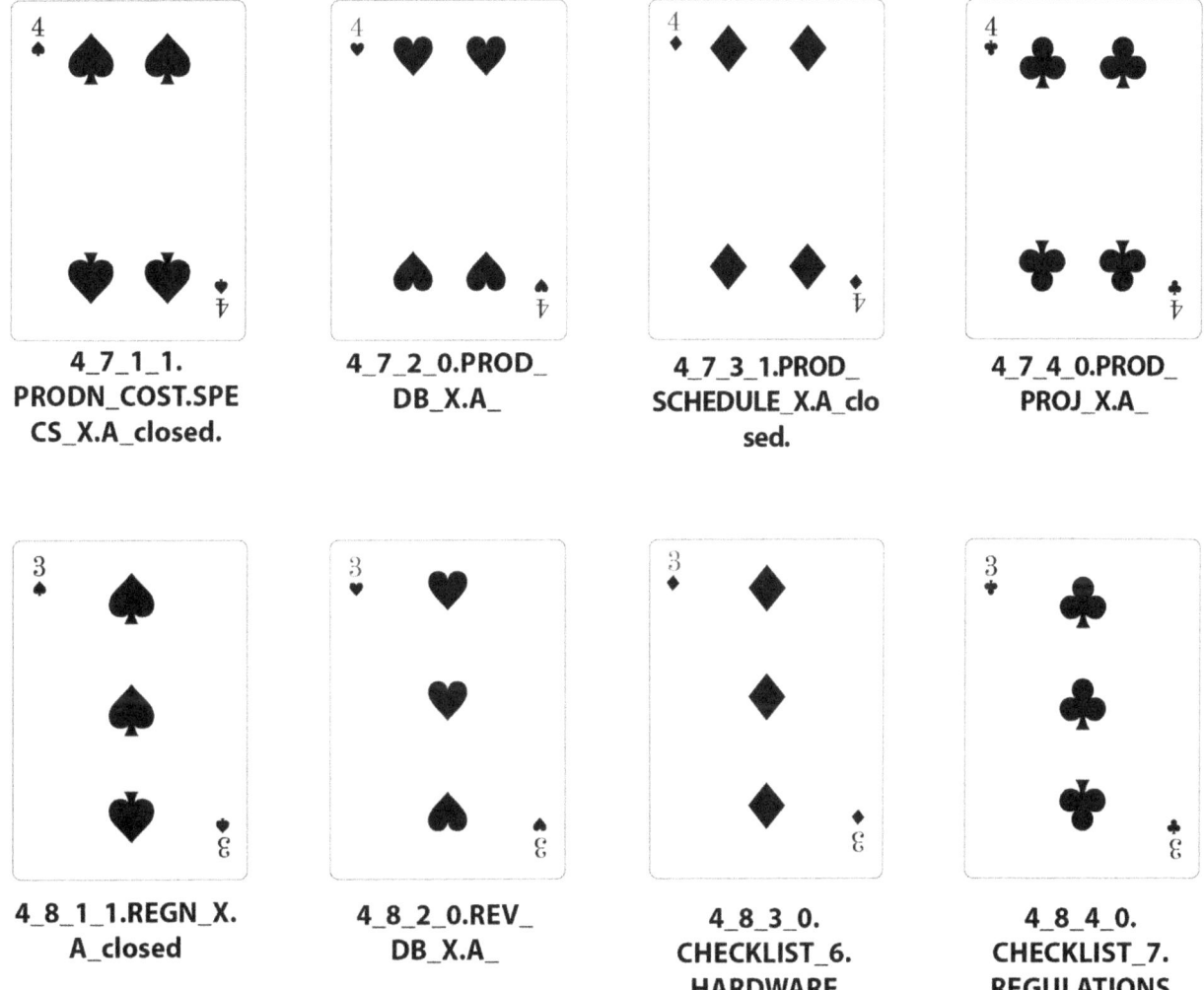

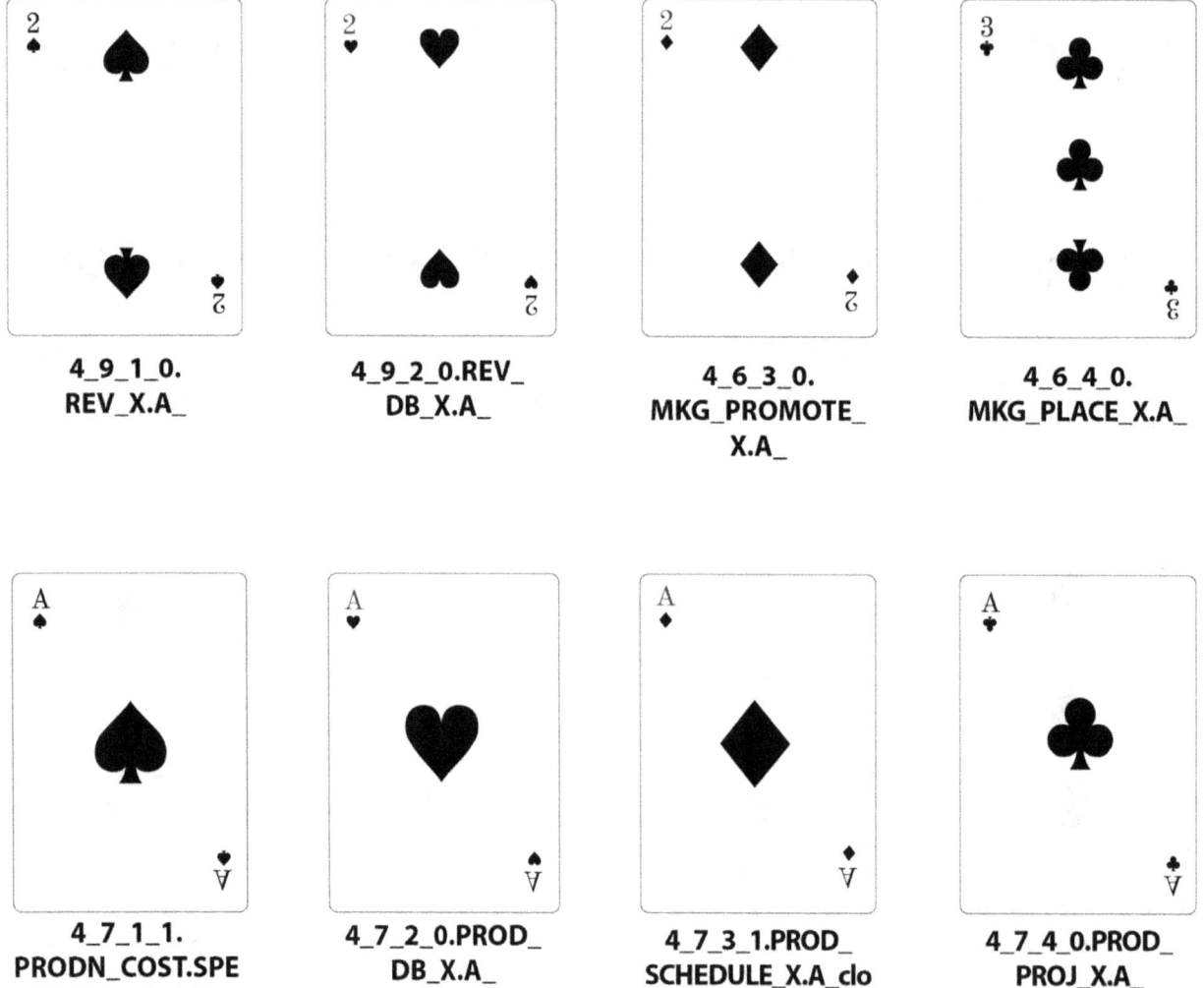

4_9_1_0.
REV_X.A_

4_9_2_0.REV_
DB_X.A_

4_6_3_0.
MKG_PROMOTE_
X.A_

4_6_4_0.
MKG_PLACE_X.A_

4_7_1_1.
PRODN_COST.SPE
CS_X.A_closed.

4_7_2_0.PROD_
DB_X.A_

4_7_3_1.PROD_
SCHEDULE_X.A_clo
sed.

4_7_4_0.PROD_
PROJ_X.A_

OBJECT:

The object of the game is to pick a fresh card from the deck or from the preceding discarded card to swap with a card on hand so as to be the first to complete one of the ten-card winning combination as follows:

MODE OF WINNING COMBINATIONS:

Card Mahjong - 70 points (default mode) or;

Bonus Mahjong with a set (triplet or quadruplet) from Royal suit or Checklists (as opted) - 100 points or;

Super-Bonus Mahjong with one declared set (as opted) - 150 points

Consolation prize:

10 points; (for displayed triplet);

20 points: (for displayed quadruplet)

5 points: (to the winning of the outright winner for answering correctly the name of the core task of the next card picked and shown from the deck).

PROCEDURE OF PLAY:

After dealing out the cards, the starting player will begin the game by drawing a fresh card from the deck (no discarded to pick yet) which he may keep or discard. Should he retain the drawn card, he would exchange it with one on hand so as to complete a winning ten-card combination comprising either (a) two sets of quadruplets plus one duet (4-4-2) or (b) two sets of triplets plus one quadruplet (4-3-3). The added fun of this game is that each player has the option to bid for playing either the "Bonus Mahjong" mode (signifying Leveraging of Resource) for a score of 100 points or for the "Super-Bonus Mahjong" mode (signifying Knowledge Application) for 150 points. Each set (of duet, triplet or quadruplet) is from a same suit which needs not be in any (spade>heart>diamond>club) order. Upon failure to win the Bonus Mahjong or Super-Bonus Mahjong as opted, the bidder player will incur a penalty of 50 points. Where there is no bidder for either option the players concerned will proceed to play for the default Card Mahjong mode. In the event of no outright win at the second deck of cards, the players with displayed set (as explained below) stand to secure a consolation point each (signifying Exercise of Strategies). The play will continue with the second deck of shuffled 52 cards if there is no outright winner at the end of the first deck.

After the starting player has discarded a card, any player by priority of being nearest to and who is able to form a triplet/quadruplet with the preceding discarded card may jump the order of play to pick it in exchange for one on hand in which event the intercepter needs to display the set of triplet or quadruplet formed on the table.

After an interception for picking and displaying of a discarded card (signifying "strategy"), the turn will go back to the player intercepted who is now the only one entitled to pick the latest discarded card. The player able to complete the "Card Mahjong", "Bonus or Super-Bonus options" has priority over any discarded card to win the game but he must declare "Win" and reveal the outright winning mode. In the event there is no outright winner, at the second deck, the players with displayed sets are entitled to a consolation of 10 points for any triplet or 20 points for any quadruplet. An outright winner has the option to name the core task on the next card picked from the deck. If he names the core task correctly, he stands to win 5 additional points on top of his outright win.

ORDER OF CARDS:

The cards are ranked in the descending order of King, Queen, Jack, Ten, Nine, Eight, Seven, Six, Five, Four, Three, Two, Ace. Within each suit, the descending order of cards is: (Spade, Heart, Diamond and Club). Ten of the rank cards, are designated "Checklist" cards. (See CARD TABLE in APPENDIX C).

Thus, through practicing the OSP Business Card (Mahjong) Game, players can be effectively trained on the competency of OSP knowledge application. They will know their core tasks and how to execute abstract concepts of wisdom, trust, courage, compassion and discipline in three steps, correlated to the core tasks to reap the biggest benefits of knowledge application. The HR may assess Staff on competency via the point score itself.

APPENDIX C

OBJECTIVE-STEPS PROCESSING TEMPLATE

CORE_TASK TABLE (CAPITALISED)

ADMINISTRATION

    1_4_1_0. AGENDA_X.A_

    1_4_2_0. AGENDA_DB.A_MINUTES

    1_4_3_0. AGENDA_MATTER_ ARISING.A_

    1_4_4_0. AGENDA_PROJ_X.A_

    2_4_1_0. ENQ_X.A_

    2_4_2_0.ENQ_ DB_X.A_

    2_4_3_0.ENQ_X. A_

    2_4_4_0. CHECKLIST_1. PAYMENT

    3_4_1_0. CONT_X.A_

    3_4_2_0. CONT_DB_X.A_

3_4_3_0.CONT_X.A_

3_4_4_0. CHECKLIST_2. TERMS_OPERATION

4_1_1_0.ACC_ POSTING_X.A_

4_1_2_0.ACC_STM_X.A_

4_1_3_0. ACC_INVOICE_X.A_

4_1_4_0. ACC_JOURNAL_X.A_

4_2_1_0.ENF_ PROCESSES_X.A_

4_2_2_0.ENF_DB_X.A_

4_2_3_0. CHECKLIST_3. TECHNICAL

4_2_4_0. CHECKLIST_4. SOURCING

4_3_1_0. FAC_ INSPECTION_X.A_

4_3_2_0.FAC_ DB_X.A_

4_3_3_0.FAC_ SERVICING_X.A_

4_3_4_0. CHECKLIST_5. SOFTWARE

4_4_1_0.GEN_ SUPV_X.A_

4_4_2_0.GEN_ DB_X.A_

4_4_3_0.GEN_ PROCESSES_X.A_

4_4_4_0.GEN_ PROJ_X.A_

4_5_1_0.HR_ RECRUIT_X.A_

4_5_2_0.HR_ DB_X.A_

4_5_3_0.HR_ REMUNERATION_ CAREER_DEV_X.A_

4_5_4_0.HR_ APPRAISAL_X.A_

4_6_1_0. MKG_PRICE_PROD_X.A_

4_6_2_0. MKG_DB_X.A_

4_6_3_0. MKG_PROMOTE_X.A_

4_6_4_0. MKG_PLACE_X.A_

4_7_1_1. PRODN_COST.SPECS_X.A_closed.

4_7_2_0.PROD_ DB_X.A_

4_7_3_1.PROD_ SCHEDULE_X.A_closed.

4_7_4_0.PROD_ PROJ_X.A_

4_8_1_1.REGN_X.A_closed

4_8_2_0.REV_ DB_X.A_

4_8_3_0. CHECKLIST_6. HARDWARE

4_8_4_0. CHECLIST_7. REGULATIONS

4_9_1_0. REV_X.A_

4_9_2_0.REV_ DB_X.A_

4_9_3_0. CHECKLIST_8. LAWS.

4_9_4_0. CHECKLIST_9. OPPORTUNITY.

4_10_1_0. SERV_X.A_

4_10_2_0. SERV_DB_X.A_

4_10_3_0. SERV_PROJ_X.A_

4_10_4_0. CHECKLIST_10. OPPORTUNITY_ OUTSOURCE

As shown in the above-listed Core Task Table (In Capitals), OSP is set up in three steps of administration and ten departments of operation. Each step/department is designated with four core tasks. Thus, the steps are correlated to core tasks extended by underscore to actual tasks and rendered executable with monitoring and correction of variances via the simple user-friendly result-targeting task-lines as shown in the format below:

COMPLETE TASK-LINE

(task code.object.attribute)

FORMAT OF DIGITAL TASK_CODE

Part-1: Task-code (for auto-filing, and quick retrieval)

Part-2: Object (Step/Department)

Part-3: Attribute (Extended to specific task by underscore)

Part-4 (Status, 0:'variance; '1': closed)

FORMAT OF TASK-LINES

4_4_3_1. gen_processes_ OSP_training_X.A_$

2_4_2_0. enq_DB_X_tender.A_$

3_4_2_0. cont_invest_proj_X.A_$

4_1_1_1. acc_posting_X.A_ error_corrected

4_2_1_0.enf_ processes_OSP_X.A_

4_3_1_0.fac_ inspection_X.A_BESTP_date

4_4_2_0. gen_DB_X.A_item

4_5_1_0.HR_recruit_post_X.A_ qualification_date

4_6_1_0. mkg_price_product_X.A_margin_%

4_7_3_0.prod_ schedule_valueAdd_X.A_Cost$

4_7_1_0.prod_ material_specs_X.A_$

4_8_1_0. reg_X.A_breach$

4_9_2_0. rev_DB_X.A_debt_$

4_10_1_0. serv_micro_agro. export_X.A_$

2_4_4_0. checklist_1. payment_ defects.

4_10_4_0. checklist_10. opportunities_ outsourcing_X

4_9_4_0. checklist_9. opportunity_ researches.

4_9_3_0. checklist_8. opportunity_ production

4_4_3_0.gen_ Processes_form_X.A_OSP_update_

4_2_1_0. enf_processes_OSP_X.A_item

The above-listed examples are selected randomly to test readers' understanding of the syntax, and core tasks. For consistency, OSP is focused on monitoring of four major tasks namely: Leveraging of resource (item 3) Intuition (Checklists) and Strategies (Production/Marketing/ Services). Explanations are provided below:

ITEM 1:

General Department's first core task: Supervision is supported by its third core task: "Processes" to provide useful overall guidance on knowledge application. If the targeted results are not attained, the task-line may be updated e.g. 4_4_3_0.g_processes. OSO_training_X_failed simply for further action. If done, the task code is closed e.g., 4_4_3_1. As closing is based on result, there is no need to be unduly concerned with technicality.

ITEM 2:

The second core task for each step/department is reserved for database. Thus, processing is supported by facts and data to track performances.

ITEM 3:

The contract step's second core task (database) ensures securing of competitive tenders/quotations is targeted for action. If result is not attained, the task-line may be updated e.g., 3_4_3.0.c_invest.X_$_ Checklist_2. Terms with use of checklist to negotiate terms etc.

ITEM 4:

The Accounts department's first core task (posting) ensures proper posting to avoid potential abuses and malpractices.

ITEM 5:

The Enforcement department's first core task (OSP processes), provides overall guidance via the core task table and one-liner task-lines template ensuring integrity of the system.

ITEM 6:

The Facility Department's first core task: Inspection (Scheduled Weekly Inspections of major maintenance items) can be extended by underscore to its Attribute core task to cover diverse activities. Flexibility is essential e.g. It may be extended to practical guidance on maintenance with acronym: e.g., "BESTP" (See details below)

ITEM 7:

The General Department's second core task (database) for monitoring of software packages e.g., online portals, networking, automation systems, or AUTO-CAD etc. Where necessary, technical staff may interact among themselves to solve software engineering problems.

ITEM 8:

HR monitors its first core task (recruitment) in coordination with relevant departments on remuneration, qualification, experience for the post.

ITEM 9:

The Marketing Department implements the 4-P of marketing taught in Marketing course.

ITEMS 10 & 11:

The Production Department's third core task: Production Scheduling requires coordination among relevant departments e.g., Accounts, Facility, Marketing and Regulation Checklist_3. Technical, Checklist_4. Sourcing etc. on cost, materials, new products, specifications, regulation and value-adding.

ITEM 12:

The Regulation Department monitors potential breach of laws or regulations in coordination with relevant departments e.g., Production Department. Checklist_7. Regulations could help avoid the risks of heavy fines or law suits. Checklist_8. Laws can help to ensure fairness and justice in punishments based on facts and circumstances.

ITEM 13:

The Revenue Department monitors potential revenue leakage, to avoid cashflow and bad debts problems etc.

ITEM 14:

The Services (outsourced) Department can tap on expertise of external contractors/specialists to be competitive in the market place e.g., micro_agro projects.

ITEM 15:

10 Checklist_1. Payment (see Core Task Table) will ensure payment, according to terms, in line with the overall interests of the enterprise.

ITEM_16:

The General Department seizes an opportunity to outsource a particular IT service to outside contractor.

ITEM_17:

The General Department seizes the opportunity to direct researches on specific scientific or technical knowledge e.g., material suitable for electric vehicles! Checklist_9. Opportunity will help to ensure capitalising on opportunities in hardware, software and researches.

ITEM_18:

The General Department seizes opportunity to start applying a knowledge in production.

ITEM_19:

In order for core tasks to serve their purposes of rendering tasks recognisable and executable for knowledge application, flexibility is essential. For example, the General Department's third core task: "Processes" need to cover Forms, Software and Hardware packages. Flexibility is needed to support these various forms.

ITEM_20:

In order to serve their objectives, flexibility is essential in relating them core tasks to specific task by underscore (_) e.g., 4_1_1_0. a_posting.error_item_X_amount_$.

As can be seen from the above-listed random example task-lines, it is essential to note that as long as staff know what are their core tasks and what needs to be done, the purpose is served. The chief executive need not know the details. All that he needs to do is to be a Servant Leader enabling staff to follow up with execution of policies/decisions made thanks to the setting of core tasks.

For example, the Facility Department is not at the mercy of forgetfulness or ad hoc practices It can proactively schedule its first core task: inspection on major maintenance items extended by underscore to acronym: e.g., B.E.S.T.P for "(B)ody, (E)lement, (S)tarter, (T)orque and (P)arts". This allows the enterprise to follow up with periodic servicing via its third core task: servicing complete with quantitative condition reading of switchgears, and moving parts. It will ensure that public transportation i.e., MRT trains, vessels, planes etc. are efficiently maintained and serviced based on schedule displayed at workplace. Upon completion, the task-line is simply closed as 4_3_1_1 (auto-filed by the spreadsheet). There is no reason for public safety and convenience to be at the mercy of talk-only conceptual practices, forgetfulness.

Various Human Resource organisations have been implemented for decades with the objective or promoting skills, good corporate governance, creativity and productivity. However, HR Department is generally run on conceptual approaches.

The HR Department may rest assured that it could now conduct recruitment based on pre-approved qualification/skill criteria with executable processes. Under its first core task it could look forward to engage talent objectively. It may follow up its third core task-remuneration/career-development to develop and retain talent. In this way, there would be transparency and accountability in appraisal of staff performance (fourth core task). These core tasks are carried out in coordination with Enforcement Department to ensure success in human resource development.

The Marketing Department will be able to implement its third (4-P) taught in marketing courses via its first and third core tasks with ease: (4.6.1.0, 4.6.3.0) verified by task line e.g., 4.6.1.0-mkt-product_material_cost_$_price result.

The Regulation Department, may coordinate with the Facility Department" first core task for compliance with crucial fire and workplace safety under the law via simple task-line's Attribute set with acronym e.g. FIRE-SAVE-HANDLE standing for "(f)ire alarm", "(r)inging bell", "(s)moke detector", "(v)oice system", "air (h)andling", "(n)otifying", "(d)oor-closer", "(l)ift-homing". Such hands-on management will ensure that commercial buildings would be functioning efficiently without forgetfulness, compromises, ad hoc and fight-fight practices.

The Services (Outsource) Department, holds the key to competitiveness. Under the second step of administration, task-line could be set with relevant Attribute guided by acronym like M.I.S.T.A.K.E.: (m)isuse of facility, (i)ntruder, (s)tealing, (t)raffic control, (a)lteration works, (k)ontractor activities and (e)rrors! Such hands-on management would go a long way towards securing the most competitive security and IT service providers etc.

SUMMARY

In summary, OSP knowledge application processes, enable businesses and governments to be run competitively with transparency and accountability by highly hands-on, effective and implementable execution. It is possible to preempt abuses and malpractices, the common cause of business/government failures. OSP therefore offers the long-awaited solution to our immense intractable human problems. Let the holistic results speak for themselves as epitomized by the OSP BYWORD: "Change, just do it".

TEST QUESTIONS:

CHAPTER ONE:

Qn:1.1:

What are the three steps of administration in OSP Knowledge Application as described in this book?

Qn:1.2:

How to correlate the three steps of administration to departmental core tasks to render abstract concepts and fuzzy tasks recognisable and executable in OSP Knowledge Application?

Qn:1.3:

How do you render abstract conceptual secret recipe executable?

CHAPTER TWO:

Qn:2.1:

How does OSP Knowledge Application Process help to circumvent or change our egoistic conceptual mindset?

CHAPTER THREE:

Qn:3.1:

What is the role of one-liner task-lines in OSP Knowledge Application?

CHAPTER FOUR:

Qn:4.1:

Why is auto-filing pivotal to OSP Knowledge Application?

CHAPTER FIVE & APPENDIX C:

Qn:4.2:

Define the OSP result-targeting one-liner task-line.

Qn:5.1:

Why should the executives be focused on attaining results for the four major tasks?

Qn:5.2:

Give an example task-line of knowledge application in Facility Department!

Qn:5.3:

Give an example task-line of knowledge application in a Production Department!

Qn: 5.4:

Give an example task-line to effect coordination between a scientist and the rest of team in a start-up enterprise!

Qn: 5.5:

Give an example task-line for just and equitable administration of laws!

Qn: 5.6

Assuming you are currently running a business and have decided to implement OSP Knowledge Application, as described in this book, how would you monitor your financial performance as described in this book?

CHAPTER SIX:

Qn: 6.1:

Describe the major benefits of OSP Knowledge Application!

CHAPTER SEVEN:

Qn 7:

What are the Four Major Tasks the executives should focus on in order to stay consistent in OSP Knowledge Application?

ANSWERS:

Ans: 1.1:

The three steps of administration in the context of knowledge application refer to the usual corporate practice of overseeing results via: (1) Agenda (proposal), (2) Enquiry (study, quotation, tender) and (3) Contract (result) steps.

Ans: 1.2:

In order to enable knowledge application, the three steps of administration should be correlated to departmental core tasks to make tasks recognisable and executable and additionally, the core tasks should be extended by underscore to cover the actual tasks so that the performance can be verified by the one-liner result-targeting task-lines.

Ans: 1.3:

To render abstract concepts in Sun Tzu Art of War executable, we need to make tasks recognisable and executable by correlating core tasks to three steps or administration (1) Agenda (2) Enquiry (3) Contract and (4) ten departments of operation followed by monitoring and correcting variances via the unique one-liner task-lines closed by knowledge application and results.

Ans: 2.1:

Concepts like leadership, meritocracy and creativity etc. are ideas or principles often employed for presentation purposes. However, they are generic varying according to individual perception and not easily implementable. Therefore in knowledge application, we need to render concepts executable with monitoring and correction of variances via the factual result-targeting execution processes.

Ans: 3.1:

As a task defined in computer science is an object set by its own in-built methods and attributes, it effectively means almost anything. There is therefore an overwhelming need to make tasks recognisable and executable. By correlating the three corporate steps of administration to departmental core tasks and actual tasks monitored by the one-liner monitoring task-lines, in effect we are rendering tasks recognisable and executable in knowledge application.

Ans: 4.1:

In the context of knowledge application, the three steps of administration are correlated to departmental core tasks coupled to one-liner result-targeting task-lines. This correlation render tasks executable supported by an auto-filing and quick retrieval system for corrective actions.

Ans:4.2:

OSP result-targeting one-liner task-line is a representation of task prefixed by a 4_part digital task code to an object followed by an attribute with underscore linking to actual task to facilitate result-closing.

Ans: 5.1:

In knowledge application it is essential to be consistent and focused in processing of execution process. For this read on the executives should be more concerned with overseeing of results on four major tasks namely leveraging of resource knowledge application, intuition and strategies.

Ans: 5.2:

By scheduling and carrying out Inspection Core Task: for rotational inspection of vulnerable items on weekly basis, verified by the one-liner task-line e.g., 4_3_1_0.f_inspection. Item part reading X_ faulty, we are essentially applying knowledge ensuring efficient facility services.

Ans: 5.3:

By carrying out Production Department's First Core Task according to specification: as monitored by task-line e.g. 4_7_1_0.p_id.item_X_ specs, we are ensuring quality customer service with our knowledge.

Ans: 5.4:

By monitoring the Production Department's Third Core Task: Scheduling as shown in the task-line e.g. 4_7_3_0.p_scheduling.iyem_X_demand_cost_?, the Accounts, Marketing and HR departments could contribute their inputs.

Ans: 5.5:

To ensure just and equitable administration of laws a typical task-line can be used to oversee sentencing e.g. 4_7_1_0.p_law_x. sentencing_checklist_8_facts_circumstances.0.

Ans: 5.6:

Set up the second core task (database) under the Accounts Depart to track your financial performance for two to three successive years as follows:

| YEAR: | TOTAL REVENUE: | PROFIT: | PERCENT: |

Compare the performance after OSP implementation with that of previous financial years. To be objective, join an OSP club to ensure proper implementation of OSP before comparisons of financial results.

Ans: 6.1:

The major benefits of OSP Knowledge Application Process include: (1) Productivity - e.g., Preventions of frequent breakdowns of facilities and public transportations due to ad hoc fire-fight management practices. (2) Knowledge Application - turning of passive knowledge into products and services. (3) Solution to immense intractable human problems of abuses and malpractices with transparency and accountability. (The actual scope can be much wider as elaborated in Appendix A).

Ans: 7.1:

For consistency in OSP Knowledge Application, it is essential to focus on the following four major tasks: (1) Leveraging on Resource (2) Knowledge Application (3) Intuition (4) Strategies.